Uniquely
Florida

Bob Knotts

Heinemann Library
Chicago, Illinois

Designed by Heinemann Library
Page layout by Wilkinson Design
Printed and bound in the United States by
Lake Book Manufacturing, Inc.

07 06 05 04
10 9 8 7 6 5 4 3 2

**Library of Congress
Cataloging-in-Publication Data**

Knotts, Bob.
    Uniquely Florida / Bob Knotts.
        p. cm. -- (State studies)
Summary: Provides an overview of various aspects
of Florida that make it a unique state, including its
land, plants and animals, people, and culture.
Includes bibliographical references (p.47) and
index.
    ISBN 1-40340-351-1 -- ISBN 1-40340-567-0
(pbk.)
    1. Florida--Juvenile literature. [1. Florida.] I. Title.
II. State
studies (Heinemann Library (Firm))
    F311.3 .K585 2002
    975.9--dc21
                                                    2002005712

Acknowledgments
The author and publishers are grateful to the
following for permission to reproduce copyright
material:

Cover photographs by (top, L-R) Hans
Deryk/AP/Wide World Photos, Joseph Sohm/Visions
of America/Corbis, Morton Beebe/Corbis, Steven J.
Nesius/Heinemann Library; (main) Brandon D.
Cole/Corbis

title (L-R) Nik Wheeler/Corbis, Mark
Newman/Photo Researchers, Jeff Foott/Bruce
Coleman; contents Stephen J. Nesius/Heinemann
Library; p. 4 Visit Florida; pp. 5, 41, 45 maps.com/
Heinemann Library; pp. 8, 15, 35, 36, 41, 42
Stephen J. Nesius/Heinemann Library;p. 9 Joseph
Sohm/Visions of America/Corbis; p. 10 One Mile
Up; p. 12 Lelcagraphie M. Serraillier/Photo
Researchers; p. 13 Karen Havenstein/Low Country
Geologic; p. 14 Julie Eggers/Bruce Coleman, Inc.;
p. 17 Jeff Foott/Bruce Coleman, Inc.; p. 18 Laura
Riley/Bruce Coleman, Inc.; pp. 19, 24, 32, 39 Tony
Arruza; p. 20 Chris O'Meara/AP/Wide World
Photos; p. 22 Mark Foley/AP/Wide World Photos;
p. 23 Werner Bertsch/Bruce Coleman, Inc.;
p. 25 Patrick Ward/Corbis; pp. 26, 34, 43B Len
Kaufman; p. 28 Free Library of Philadelphia,
Philadelphia, Pennsylvania/Scala/Art Resource;
p. 29 Smithsonian Museum of American Art,
Washington, D.C./Art Resource; p. 30 Bettmann/
Corbis; p. 31 Dave G. Houser/Corbis; p. 37 New
World Symphony; p. 38 Greg Fight/Tampa
Tribune/Silver Image; p. 40 Nik Wheeler/Corbis;
p. 43T Dave G. Houser/Corbis; p. 44 Mark
Newman/Photo Researchers

Photo Research by Julie Laffin

Special thanks to Charles Tingley of the St. Augustine
Historical Society for his comments in the
preparation of this manuscript.

Every effort has been made to contact copyright
holders of any material reproduced in this book.
Any omissions will be rectified in subsequent
printings if notice is given to the publisher.

Some words are shown in bold, **like this.**
You can find out what they mean by looking
in the glossary.

Contents

Uniquely Florida

What does it mean to be unique? Unique describes anything that is different in some important way from everything else in the world, or something that is one of a kind. For example, there is no one else on Earth who is exactly like you, which makes you unique.

Places and things can be unique, too. Nowhere else in the world is exactly like Florida. The land, plants, animals, and people are all part of what makes Florida unique.

Florida is a land of sunshine, beaches, and warm weather. The Sunshine State has many unique places to explore.

LOCATION

Florida's location **influences** its weather. The state is in the far southeastern corner of the

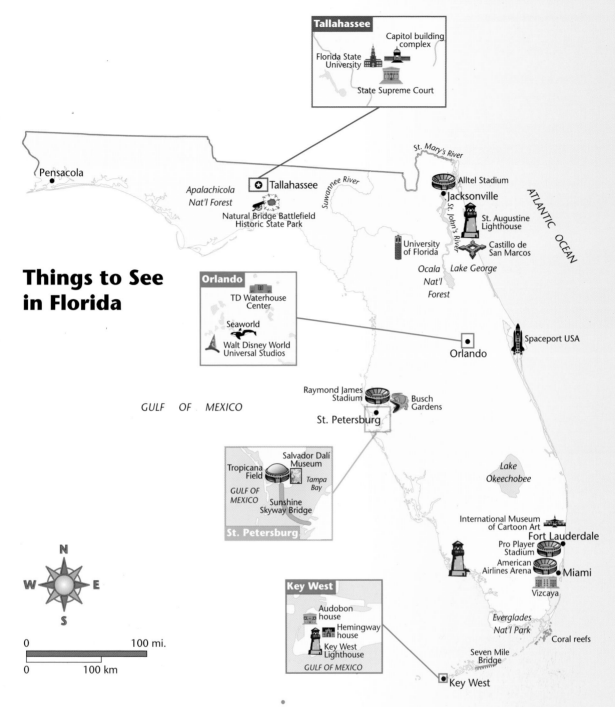

Things to See in Florida

Tallahassee
- Florida State University
- Capitol building complex
- State Supreme Court

Pensacola

Apalachicola Nat'l Forest

Tallahassee

Suwannee River

St. Mary's River

Alltel Stadium
Jacksonville
St. Augustine Lighthouse
Castillo de San Marcos

ATLANTIC OCEAN

Natural Bridge Battlefield Historic State Park

University of Florida

St. John's River

Ocala Nat'l Forest

Lake George

Orlando
- TD Waterhouse Center
- Seaworld
- Walt Disney World
- Universal Studios

Orlando

Spaceport USA

GULF OF MEXICO

Raymond James Stadium
Busch Gardens
St. Petersburg

Lake Okeechobee

St. Petersburg
- Tropicana Field
- Salvador Dalí Museum
- GULF OF MEXICO
- Tampa Bay
- Sunshine Skyway Bridge

International Museum of Cartoon Art
Fort Lauderdale
Pro Player Stadium
American Airlines Arena
Miami
Vizcaya

Everglades Nat'l Park

Coral reefs

Key West
- Audobon house
- Hemingway house
- Key West Lighthouse
- GULF OF MEXICO

Seven Mile Bridge

Key West

N W E S

| 0 | 100 mi. |
| 0 | 100 km |

United States. The Atlantic Ocean borders Florida's eastern shores; the Gulf of Mexico is on the state's western and southern coastlines; the state of Georgia is to Florida's north; and the state of Alabama is to Florida's north and northwest (map page 45). Aside from Hawaii, Florida is the southern-most state in the country.

Many of Florida's attractions, such as Seaworld, are known all around the world.

How Southern Is Southern?

Florida is the southernmost state in the continental United States. Key West is only 90 miles from Cuba. Florida's **latitude** runs from 24°30' N to 31° N; Florida's **longitude** runs from 79°48' W to 87°38' W.

Look at a globe. The **circumference** of the Earth is divided into 360 degrees. On a globe, each degree is shown as an imaginary line running from the north to the south, or the east to the west. The **equator,** an imaginary horizontal line, is what divides the Northern Hemisphere from the Southern Hemisphere. The **prime meridian,** an imaginary vertical line, is what divides the Eastern Hemisphere from the Western Hemisphere. Try to locate Florida on a globe and find its latitude and longitude.

Florida is the most **tropical** state in the **continental** United States. The sun shines more than 300 days a year here. Temperatures are fairly warm all year long, and many plants **thrive** in this weather. Some of Florida's plants, like the scrub palm, live no place else on Earth.

FLORIDIANS

People who live in Florida are called Floridians. Today, Floridians can trace their **ancestors** to over 250 countries around the world. Many Floridians like the sunny weather, sandy beaches, and warm ocean water in this state. Many also like Florida because it is close to other countries to the south and east. These countries include Jamaica, Haiti, Cuba, Venezuela, and Colombia. People from these and many other countries live in Florida partly because it is near their homeland.

Lightning Capital

Florida is the lightning capital of the United States. Because of its warm, wet weather, the state receives more lightning strikes and has more lightning injuries and deaths than anywhere else in the nation.

From 1959 to 1999, lightning injured or killed 1,855 people in Florida. The state with the second highest number of lightning injuries or deaths during that time was Michigan, with 772. Florida had more than twice that number.

They come to the United States seeking a better life, but still like to visit their families back home.

Florida is the fourth most populated state in the United States. Only California, Texas, and New York have more people than Florida. Floridians have many different customs and eat a wide variety of foods. They enjoy many different types of music,

Over the past ten years, Florida's people have changed. Which group grew the most? Which group shrank in the overall population?

Florida's Demographics: 1990 vs. 2000

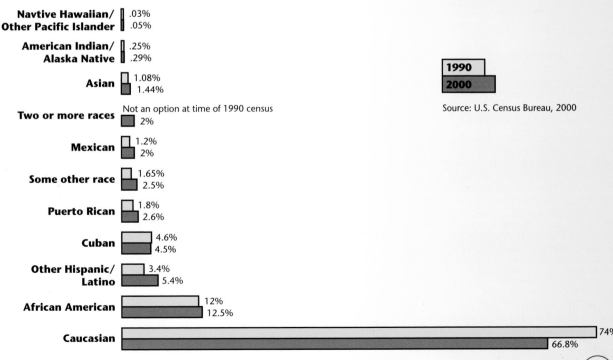

Navtive Hawaiian/ Other Pacific Islander — .03% / .05%

American Indian/ Alaska Native — .25% / .29%

Asian — 1.08% / 1.44%

Two or more races — Not an option at time of 1990 census / 2%

Mexican — 1.2% / 2%

Some other race — 1.65% / 2.5%

Puerto Rican — 1.8% / 2.6%

Cuban — 4.6% / 4.5%

Other Hispanic/ Latino — 3.4% / 5.4%

African American — 12% / 12.5%

Caucasian — 74% / 66.8%

1990
2000

Source: U.S. Census Bureau, 2000

The Hillsboro Point Lighthouse was built in 1906. The City of Lighthouse Point takes its name from this structure. Florida is well-known for its many lighthouses.

sports, and art. Florida is unique partly because the state offers so many different things from around the world, all in one place. Together with Florida's land areas, plants, animals, and weather, its people help make this state unique.

There are more reasons why Florida is unique. Florida has many unique buildings, lighthouses, bridges, theme parks, and museums. It also has its own songs, stories, recipes, and more.

To take a tour that explores this unique side of Florida, just keep reading. Florida's fun and fascinating facts are just waiting to be revealed. You will soon discover your own list of favorite things in America's Sunshine State.

Florida State Symbols

STATE FLAG

Many flags have flown over Florida's sunny land throughout its history. These include the flags of five countries: Spain, France, Great Britain, the Confederate States of America (during the United States **Civil War)**, and the United States.

Florida's current flag became an official part of the state in 1900. It has a white background with the state seal in the center. The state seal is a drawing that represents Florida. A large red "X" crosses the flag as well. This "X" was added to the flag so that it never looks like a white flag of **truce** when hanging from a pole.

Florida's state flag flies proudly over government buildings and many businesses in the state. If you look closely, you will see Florida's state seal in the center of the flag.

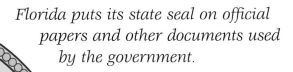

Florida puts its state seal on official papers and other documents used by the government.

STATE SEAL

Florida's state seal was first used in 1868. Some details in the seal's drawing have changed over the years to make it look more like the real Florida. These include changing the drawing of the Native American woman on the seal. Before the change, this woman looked like she was from a group in the western United States. Now, she looks like a Florida Seminole woman.

The state seal shows the woman standing by water. The sun's rays are spread across the sky. A sabal, or cabbage, palm tree grows near the woman, and a steamboat sails on the water. Around the rim of the seal are these words: "Great Seal Of The State Of Florida. In God We Trust."

The woman stands for Florida's earliest people, the Native Americans. The water and tree are meant to look like **tropical** places that are common in Florida. The boat shows an early form of transportation in Florida. The sun helps to show what a beautiful, hopeful place Florida can be.

STATE MOTTO

A motto is a short saying that means something special. Florida's motto is on its flag and seal: "In God We Trust." This motto became part of the state seal in 1868. This same motto is common around our country. In fact, the United States uses this motto on all its **currency.** Before "In God We Trust" was used in Florida, the state had a slightly different motto. It once said, "In God Is Our Trust."

STATE NICKNAME

In 1970 the Florida **legislature** picked the state's official nickname, the "Sunshine State," which is still used today. This name had been used unofficially since 1949 on Florida's license plates. The nickname is meant to tell everyone in just a few words about Florida's weather. Florida has more than 300 days of sunshine each year!

STATE SONG

Florida's state song is "Swanee River" (also known as "Old Folks At Home"). The song was written by one of the most famous American songwriters of the 1800s, Stephen C. Foster. Foster wrote the song about the river in 1851, and the song soon became very popular. "Swanee River" was adopted as Florida's official song in 1935.

The Florida river's name is actually spelled differently: the Suwannee River. It runs from Georgia's Okefenokee Swamp, just north of Florida, to the Gulf of Mexico on Florida's west coast. Foster never actually visited the Suwannee River, or even the state of Florida. He just liked the name "Swanee" so much that he used it for his song.

"Swanee River"

Did you ever wonder why Florida's state song is called "Swanee River" ("Old Folks At Home")? Who are the "old folks" in the song? The song's opening words help explain the title:

> "Way down upon the Swanee River
> Far, far, away
> That's where my heart is turning ever,
> There's where the old folks stay."

The "old folks" are family, and the song is about the comfort of home and family.

STATE PLAY

The state play of Florida is called *The Cross and Sword*. This **drama** tells the story of early European settlers who came to Florida. It tells how these settlers founded the oldest permanent European city in the state, St. Augustine, on Florida's northeast coast. The play, written by Paul Green, was officially chosen to be the state play in 1973. It was performed during the summer months in St. Augustine for over 25 years.

STATE SOIL

The Florida **legislature** picked myakka *(my-yak-ah)* fine sand as the state **soil** in 1989. Myakka fine sand is a tan-colored sand found only in Florida. This is Florida's most common soil. It covers more than 1.5 million acres in the state.

STATE GEM

Florida's state gem, the moonstone, is one of its strangest state symbols. It was chosen as the state gem in 1970. This was the year after Apollo 11 took off from the Kennedy Space Center in Florida to land humans on the moon for the first time in history.

Many people think moonstones are an odd choice for Florida's state gem because they cannot be found naturally in Florida!

Agatized coral is much rarer than other types of coral. It takes 20 to 30 million years for agatized coral to form.

Because the Kennedy Space Center is in Florida, the state legislature wanted to pay honor to the successful mission to the moon. This is why they picked the moonstone. However, the moonstone does not come from the moon. Also, it is not found anywhere in Florida! It can be found in the states of Pennsylvania and Virginia.

STATE STONE

Agatized coral was picked as the state stone in 1979. This coral is found in four main places within Florida, all near the Gulf of Mexico: the Econfina River and the bottoms of the Suwannee and Withlacoochee Rivers, in northwest Florida, and in Tampa Bay, on Florida's west coast.

Two Rivers, One Name

Florida is the only state with two rivers that share the same name. There is a Withlacoochee River in central Florida, and another Withlacoochee River in northern Florida. They are not connected in any way except by name.

Coral comes from tiny sea animals called polyps. Many of these creatures live together in saltwater. They form hard shells outside their bodies. These shells can be found in beautiful shapes and colors and are called coral.

Agatized coral slowly takes shape when a kind of quartz forms from material in the saltwater and takes over the shape of the original coral. This new stone is called a pseudomorph *(sue-doe-morf)*, which means that one kind of mineral replaced another kind without losing its original shape.

STATE SHELL

In 1969, the horse conch was named Florida's official shell. This shell can be as long as 24 inches, and is found in the sea off Florida's coasts. It is also known as the giant band shell.

STATE TREE

The sabal palm has been Florida's state tree since 1953. This tree is also called the cabbage palm. It is one of the most common trees in the state.

STATE FLOWER

In 1909, the orange blossom was named Florida's official flower. The white blossoms have a very pleasant smell. It is interesting to note that the orange blossom is not native to Florida, but was chosen as the state flower because of the importance of oranges to the state's economy.

STATE WILDFLOWER

The coreopsis became the state wildflower in 1991.

Florida's state wildflower, the coreopsis, comes in many colors, including pink and gold.

Many of these flowers have been planted along Florida's roads to make the state look prettier for motorists.

STATE BEVERAGE

What drink would make the perfect state beverage of Florida? Orange juice, of course! Florida's vast orange groves bring in billions of dollars each year. Oranges are not just important to the economy. To many people, this fruit and its tasty juice are the first things that come to mind when they think of Florida. Orange juice was named the state beverage in 1967.

STATE REPTILE

Alligators are common in the Everglades and other wet areas of Florida. Like oranges, many people think of alligators when they think of Florida. For these reasons, the state **legislature** picked the alligator as the official state reptile in 1987. But long before it was official, many Floridians and visitors thought of the alligator as a state symbol.

Many visitors hope to see a "gator" during their stay in Florida. About one million alligators live in Florida.

Unofficial Ex-Litterbug

Florida has another symbol that is unofficial, but is often used to help keep the state beautiful. His name is Sticky Man. Sticky Man is a character who was once a bad litterbug until his trash began to stick to him. Now he is a superhero who tells people to avoid littering around the state.

The Sticky Man character visits schools, malls, and sporting events to remind everyone to pick up after themselves and keep Florida clean.

STATE ANIMAL

The Florida panther was named the state animal in 1982. This wild cat was picked not by state lawmakers, but by students in Florida. They voted it the animal that best represented the state. The Florida panther is on the list of animals in danger of becoming extinct. This means that so few are left alive that soon there might not be any. People in Florida are working hard to make sure this doesn't happen.

STATE SALTWATER MAMMAL

Florida named the porpoise as the state saltwater mammal in 1975, but people had trouble deciding whether to call it by the name "porpoise" or by its other name, "dolphin." They finally settled on calling it a porpoise. These gentle, intelligent animals swim very fast and often follow boats and ships at sea. They are common in the ocean waters around Florida.

STATE MARINE MAMMAL

The manatee was named the state marine mammal in 1975. These gentle, large creatures remind some people of cows. They can grow to be 14 feet long, and weigh 2,000 pounds. They live in Florida's warm springs and rivers.

STATE SALTWATER FISH

In 1975 the sailfish was named as Florida's official saltwater fish. These large fish are found off Florida's coastlines during winter months. They can grow up to 7 feet long, and can swim 60 miles per hour. Though sailfish are found in other warm areas around the world, Florida is well known as a place where people can try to catch sailfish.

Although manatees occasionally swim into the waters of nearby states during warmer months, there are more manatees in Florida throughout the year than anywhere else in the United States.

If you visit or live in Florida, you almost certainly will hear a mockingbird sing. Mockingbirds help people by eating insects. In fact, they sometimes pick insects off the front of parked cars.

STATE FRESHWATER FISH

The largemouth bass was chosen to be Florida's freshwater fish in 1975. Freshwater is water that has little or no salt in it, and is the kind of water found in most lakes and rivers. The largemouth bass grows larger in Florida than in many other areas. In Florida, this fish can weigh fifteen pounds and grow to be more than twenty inches long.

STATE BIRD

The mockingbird became Florida's state bird in 1927. These birds are known for the wide variety of songs they sing. Mockingbirds have their own unique song, but they also learn songs from other birds. They are called mockingbirds because they mock, or imitate, other birds' songs. The mockingbird is very common in Florida and throughout the southeastern United States.

STATE BUTTERFLY

There are many beautiful and colorful butterflies in Florida. The zebra longwing was named the official butterfly of Florida in 1996. This black and yellow butterfly lives throughout the state, but it is most common in the warmest areas of southern Florida.

Florida's State Government

The capital of Florida is Tallahassee, located in the panhandle. This city is the home of Florida's government. The governor and other state officials live there. Tallahassee is where the **legislature** meets each year to write new laws.

Florida's government is based on the state constitution. The current Florida constitution was adopted in 1968. The constitution explains how the government is supposed to work. The constitution also promises many freedoms for people who live in Florida. The freedoms named in Florida's constitution, such as the freedom of speech and the freedom to practice any religion, are based on the freedoms offered by the United States constitution.

Florida's constitution has made its government a lot like the **federal government** in other ways, too. Like the federal government in Washington, D.C., Florida's government has three main branches: the executive branch, the legislative branch, and the judicial branch.

EXECUTIVE BRANCH

The executive branch is the part of government that runs the state from day to day.

Many people think that Tallahassee is one of the most beautiful capital cities in the country.

The governor and the lieutenant governor, the second-highest state official, work in this part of state government. They make sure the laws are carried out properly. In Florida, the governor and lieutenant governor are elected to four-year terms of office. They are allowed to run for office again at the end of this time and can serve another four years. Florida's **cabinet** is also a part of this branch of government. The cabinet is made up of six elected officials who help the governor make decisions. This part of Florida's government is unique. No other state in the country elects a cabinet.

Florida governors, such as Jeb Bush (left), must work with many different state officials to help run the government.

LEGISLATIVE BRANCH

The legislative branch is formed by Florida's **legislature,** made up of a group of elected citizens. The legislature makes Florida's laws. There are two parts of the legislature, called the two houses, which are the Senate and the House of Representatives.

The Senate has 40 members, each of whom is elected to a four-year term. The senators come from every part of the state and are elected by Florida's citizens. The House of Representatives has 120 members, who serve two-year terms. Like the senators, the members of Florida's House are elected by local citizens and come from every corner of the state. Both the Senate and House of Representatives meet for about two months each year. They talk about ideas for new laws. Then they vote to accept or reject these ideas.

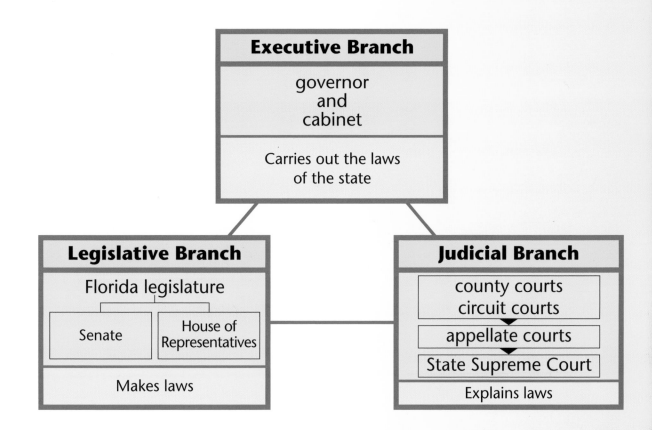

JUDICIAL BRANCH

The judicial branch of government is the court system. The courts make decisions about problems that involve Florida's laws.

The Florida State Supreme Court is the highest, or most powerful, court in Florida. The seven members of that court solve problems that have come to them from lower courts. This happens when people aren't happy with the decisions of those lower courts, and therefore decide to **appeal** their cases. In Florida, the lower courts include county courts, circuit courts, and district courts of appeals.

Some of the problems involve crimes. In these cases, the police may say that someone broke the law, while that person may say that he or she did not. The court decides who is right. Other problems involve different kinds of

Florida's State Supreme Court makes important legal decisions. Here, a lawyer argues his case before the justices, or judges, of the Florida State Supreme Court.

problems. For example, someone may owe money to another person but refuse to pay it. The court decides if the money should be paid or not.

Taxes

To keep all these branches of government running, Florida needs money. It raises money through taxes. For example, when a person buys something in Florida, he or she has to pay a little more money than the item actually costs. That extra money is called a sales tax. The store then sends the extra money to the government in Tallahassee. Florida is unique because its citizens do not have to pay **income tax** or **inheritance tax,** as people do in other states.

Florida Capitol Complex

The Capitol Complex is the center of Florida's government, and is where the **legislature** meets. The executive branch also has offices in a 22-story building that is part of this complex. The current state capitol was completed in 1977 and opened officially in 1978. The Capitol Complex looks very different from most state capitol buildings.

OLD CAPITOL

Some people prefer Florida's old capitol building, which stands nearby. The original brick building was finished in 1845, and several additions over the years made it larger. As the state government grew, however, the legislature needed an even larger place to do its work. State officials decided it was time for a new building, but they also decided to save the old building rather than tear it down.

The Capitol Complex is where the governor works. This photo shows the old capitol building in front of the new capitol building.

Today, the old capitol has red and white striped **awnings.** It is home to a number of offices and several **exhibits** on the history of Florida's government.

Early Capitol Of Logs

In 1824, Tallahassee was picked to be Florida's capital city because it was halfway between the two earlier capitals of St. Augustine and Pensacola. At that time, however, Florida's government was not yet large enough for a large, brick capitol building.

Therefore, lawmakers worked in small log cabins. Three log cabins served together as Florida's first capitol in 1824. By 1826, the state had built a tall, narrow, two-story building to replace the cabins. Florida officials intended to expand this small building, but they never did. By 1839, Florida had enough **federal** money to construct a new building. The state soon began work on the brick capitol that still stands today, and is known as the old capitol.

Music in Florida

Today's Florida has some of the most varied music in the world. There is gospel music, folk music, blues, and southern rock. There is reggae music, brought by the many Caribbean people who live in Florida today. Classical music is played at symphonies, operas, and musical theaters. Florida's Native Americans sing traditional songs during celebrations they have held for centuries.

One type of music often heard in Florida is called salsa. This is dance music played with trumpets, drums, and other instruments. When words are sung to salsa they are usually in Spanish, because salsa originally came to Florida with the Hispanic people who moved there.

These people are dancing to music at a street festival in Miami.

These tuba players are marching in the Florida Strawberry Festival Parade in Plant City. The Strawberry Festival dates back to 1930, when members of the Plant City Lyons Club had the idea for an event to celebrate the plentiful harvest of strawberries.

MUSIC FESTIVALS

White Springs, Florida, has hosted a festival called the Florida Folk Festival for over 50 years. Many talented musicians from Florida and around the country come to share their folk, blues, country, bluegrass, Latin, Caribbean, and Cajun music. The official state fiddle contest is also held there. Many people go to this festival not just to hear the music, but also to talk to the musicians and learn what makes each of these types of music unique.

Other music festivals include the Battle of the Bands, in Orlando, during which local bands play their music for large crowds. Smaller festivals, like the Strawberry Festival in Plant City, provide opportunities for local musicians and high school marching bands to play. Florida is also known for its university marching bands. For example, the Florida A & M Marching 100 have performed around the country, at the Olympics, and even in France!

From the southern rock of the band Lynyrd Skynyrd, to the bagpipe band of Dunedin, Florida, to the **spiritual** history of brothers John Rosamond Johnson and James Weldon Johnson, there are so many kinds of music in Florida that there is something for everyone to enjoy.

Florida's Food

Many types of foods are served in Florida's homes and restaurants. Some are popular because they use ingredients that are common in Florida, like stone crab or citrus fruits. Other foods, like hushpuppies, have been eaten by Florida's families for many generations. Still others were brought by **immigrants.** Just like its music, Florida's foods come from many parts of the world.

For example, most Hispanic restaurants serve black beans on top of rice. This is a dish that many people eat every day in Hispanic countries. A Caribbean dish popular in Florida is called jerked chicken. Jerked chicken is cooked in a spicy coating made from hot peppers. It makes your tongue burn!

One recipe created right in the Sunshine State is for Key lime pie. A Key lime is smaller than a normal lime, and it grows in southern Florida and the Florida Keys.

One of the most popular desserts in Florida is Key lime pie. Florida grows its own special Key limes.

26

Key Lime Pie

- 1 can (14 oz.) sweetened condensed milk
- 3 egg yolks
- 2/3 cup Key lime juice (fresh preferred)
- zest of one lime
- whipped cream

Always have an adult help you when working with the oven!

Mix the egg yolks and lime zest. Slowly add the condensed milk. Add the lime juice. Make certain that all the ingredients are mixed well. Pour into a nine-inch graham cracker pie shell. Bake in the oven at 350 degrees for about 10 minutes. Cool the pie, then refrigerate it overnight. Top with whipped cream and serve.

Ripe Key limes are yellow, not green! Above is a recipe you can use to make your own Key lime pie.

Here is a recipe for Florida-style hushpuppies. Hush-puppies are a common southern food that have been made in Florida since at least the **Civil War** (1861–1865).

Florida-Style Hushpuppies

- 2 1/2 cups coarsely ground yellow cornmeal
- 3 tablespoons flour
- 3 teaspoons double-acting baking powder
- salt and pepper, to taste
- 2 eggs plus 1 yolk, well beaten
- 1 cup water
- 1 medium onion, minced
- bacon drippings

Always make sure to have an adult work the stovetop for you!

Mix the cornmeal, flour, baking powder, salt, and pepper. Beat the eggs and yolk in another bowl until thickened. Add water and blend. Mix in the onion and salt. Next, mix the corn and egg mixtures and blend lightly. Heat the bacon drippings in a large, deep frying pan. With a spoon, scoop small balls of the corn mixture. Drop carefully into the hot pan. Fry until crisp and golden-brown on all sides, turning often. Drain on paper towels and serve hot.

Florida's Art

To many artists, Florida's unusual plants and animals are interesting to draw, paint, or sculpt. So are the state's sunsets, as well as its land and seashores. Many artists have come to Florida to create images of these things in their own way. While we cannot name them all here, the following are some of Florida's well-known artists.

JOHN JAMES AUDUBON

One of the most famous artists to work in Florida was John James Audubon. Audubon was born in 1785 in the country now known as Haiti. Audubon traveled to St. Augustine

Audubon is best known for his watercolor paintings of birds, which contain careful attention to detail. Audubon saw several flocks of American flamingos in the Florida Keys in 1832, but he did not complete this drawing until 1838.

and Key West during 1832 to work on paintings of birds. While there, he sighted and drew eighteen new birds for the large book he was writing on the birds of North America. Today, some of Audubon's work can be viewed in the Key West house where he stayed.

GEORGE INNESS JR.

George Inness Jr. was born in 1854. He became famous for painting both landscapes and animals. In the 1880s, he traveled throughout the American West making illustrations of **big game** hunts for popular magazines of the day. Many of his paintings can be seen today in Tarpon Springs, Florida, where he had his winter home.

This 1887 painting by Inness, titled September Afternoon, *shows the style he used to paint landscapes.*

THE HIGHWAYMEN

Florida was also home to a group of painters called the Highwaymen. During the 1950s, a small group of African-American men and one woman set off driving up and down Florida's east coast. They painted the landscapes they saw and sold these paintings from the trunks of their cars. Today, this kind of art is called folk art, or outsider art. This means that the art was made by people who were not trained as artists, but who used their natural skills and talents to make art that represented the way they lived and thought about the world. The Highwaymen and their art helped to inspire a particular way of painting in Florida called the Indian River school of painting.

Florida Folklore and Legends

The terms "folklore" and "folktales" describe stories that are told by one generation to the next over many years. The stories explain why something is done a certain way, or why things look the way they do. They can teach lessons or tell about an event. Legends are similar, but are told as if the events really happened.

THE 1926 HURRICANE

One folktale is about the 1926 hurricane in Miami. People said that the wind was so strong it blew a well up out of the ground, blew a crooked road straight, and scattered the days of the week so badly that Sunday didn't show up until late Tuesday morning!

A folktale was created about the force of the 1926 Miami hurricane.

GASPARILLA THE PIRATE

A Florida legend tells about the pirate Gasparilla, who terrorized Florida's west

According to legend, the real name of Gasparilla the pirate was Jose Gaspar. The legend of Gasparilla is recreated each year with a festival held in the city of Tampa.

coast during the late 1700s. He had just decided to retire when one last ship appeared—a navy ship in disguise. After fierce fighting, Gasparilla realized that the battle was lost. Instead of surrendering, he wrapped himself in an iron chain and jumped, sinking to the bottom of the ocean floor.

SEMINOLE LEGEND

A Seminole legend tells about a frog sleeping near some lilies. A rabbit hopped by and said: "Wake up! It's too nice outside to sleep!" The frog was annoyed, and replied that he didn't have anything else to do, but the rabbit kept pestering him. The frog finally got so mad that he started to sing a funny little song that he hoped would call the rain. Soon, a black cloud came and brought the rain. The rabbit got so cold and wet that he ran home. Today, whenever you hear frogs singing, you should find shelter. According to this legend, rain is coming soon!

A Floridian's Request

No one is sure who wrote this funny poem, but it tells a story that every Floridian can understand:

> Bless this house, oh please, we cry,
> Please keep it cool in mid–July.
> Bless the walls where termites dine,
> And ants and roaches march in time.
> Bless our yard where spiders pass
> Fire ant castles in the grass.
> Bless the garage, a home to please
> Carpenter beetles, ticks, and fleas.
> Bless the love bugs, two by two,
> The gnats and mosquitoes that
>   feed on you.
> Millions of creatures that fly or crawl,
> In Florida, we've got them all!
> But this is home and here we'll stay,
> So thanks a lot for insect spray!

Sports

Florida has plenty of professional sports and professional sports teams to choose from. The Florida Marlins and Tampa Bay Devil Rays play baseball; the Miami Dolphins, Jacksonville Jaguars, and Tampa Bay Buccaneers play football; the Miami Heat, Orlando Magic, Miami Sol, and Orlando Miracle play basketball; the Florida Panthers and Tampa Bay Lightning play hockey; and the Miami Fusion and Tampa Bay Mutiny play soccer.

Florida's universities also have sports teams. The Orange Bowl, Citrus Bowl, and Gator Bowl, all of which are held only in Florida, are important games in college football.

Florida's first major league baseball team, the Marlins, plays at Pro Player Stadium. The stadium is located between Fort Lauderdale and Miami on Florida's southeast coast.

WEATHER AND SPORTS

In addition to Florida's own baseball teams, the warm climate makes it the perfect place to host

Predicting the Future?

In the movie *Back to the Future 2*, people can travel through time. The movie was made during the 1980s, long before Florida had any Major League Baseball teams. In this movie, a magic book said that a Florida major league team would win the baseball World Series in 1997.

In real life, Florida finally got its first Major League Baseball team, the Florida Marlins, in 1993, long after *Back to the Future 2* was made. In 1997, the real-life Marlins did win the World Series, just as the movie predicted!

spring training camps for many other Major League Baseball teams. The Cincinnati Reds, New York Yankees, Detroit Tigers, and Kansas City Royals all take advantage of Florida's warm weather to get in shape for the season.

Florida's mild climate is the reason that many tennis and golf players choose to live here. The warm weather makes it easy for tennis stars and top golf players to practice their sports year-round. Florida's climate also makes the state perfect to host major golf tournaments, such as the PGA Player's Championship.

POLO AND CRICKET

Some of the best professional polo players in the world compete every winter near West Palm Beach. Polo is a game played on horses. Each team has four players who try to hit a small ball with a mallet, which is a long stick with a heavy end, as they ride their horses at full speed. Players try to hit the ball between two posts to score a goal. The team with the most goals at the end of the game wins.

Cricket is a popular game in some Caribbean countries, like Jamaica. It is also popular in southern Florida because

Cricket was a sport originally played in Great Britain. British settlers took the sport to the Caribbean, where it became a favorite game.

so many Jamaican Americans now live there. Cricket is much like baseball. Teams play innings and try to score runs by batting a ball. The team with the most runs wins.

WATER SPORTS

Because there is so much water in Florida, residents are able to participate in water sports such as snorkeling, scuba diving, fishing, and boating. Each year, Florida looks forward to the longest river sailboat race in the world, called the Mug Race. This race runs 42 miles, from Palatka to Jacksonville, on the St. John's River. Florida is also known for yachting. One popular yacht race found only in Florida is called the Regatta del Sol al Sol. This is a 456-mile race that takes place each year between St. Petersburg and Isla Mujeres, an island near Mexico's Yucatan Peninsula.

The International Swimming Hall of Fame, in Fort Lauderdale, sponsors swimming and diving competitions. The Hall of Fame also has a museum where visitors can learn about some of the best swimmers in history.

Cultural Highlights

Florida's universities offer high-quality education and top professors. Two universities, the University of Florida (UF) and Florida State University (FSU), are especially well known. The University of Florida is located in Gainesville, and has more than 40,000 students and 4,000 teachers. Florida State University is in Tallahassee, and has more than 34,000 students and 2,000 teachers.

Both UF and FSU prepare students for many kinds of careers. Both schools bring fine musicians and artists to their communities to teach and perform. These universities and others add a lot of life and **culture** to Florida.

ART MUSEUMS

One of Florida's important museums is the Salvador Dalí Museum in St. Petersburg.

Salvador Dalí was one of the most famous artists of the 1900s. The Dalí Museum has over 1,500 works of art, all created by Dalí.

This museum has the world's best collection of paintings and other works by this Spanish **surrealist** artist.

Boca Raton, Florida, is home to the International Museum of Cartoon Art. If you like cartoons or comic books, this is the place for you. The museum has more than 160,000 original cartoon drawings. Some are by Walt Disney. Others are by Charles Schultz, who created the *Peanuts* comic strip.

OTHER MUSEUMS

The Orlando Science Center is a good place to learn about the world around you. Its **exhibits** on lasers, body parts, the solar system, electricity, and dinosaur fossils help students of all ages understand more about ourselves, the history of our world, and our **environment.**

The Ringling Museum of the Circus in Sarasota covers the history of the circus. It displays posters, equipment, clothing, and **props** that have been used in the circus over the past 200 years. Also in Sarasota is the Ringling Museum of Art, which contains paintings by many famous American and European artists.

The Ringling Museum of the Circus was established in 1948. It was the first of its kind to display the history of the circus in the United States.

The New World Symphony in Miami is led by famous conductor Michael Tilson Thomas.

There are many more museums in Florida where you can learn about the state's history, animals, plants, and art. The Florida Museum of Natural History in Gainesville has over 25 million **specimens,** and is the largest natural history museum in the southeastern United States. The Allyn Museum of Entomology in Sarasota has the world's third-largest collection of butterflies and moths. The Museum of Florida History in Tallahassee has 44,000 historical **artifacts** and sponsors a number of educational programs. The Charles Hosmer Morse Museum of American Art in Winter Park has one of the world's largest collections of art by Louis Comfort Tiffany, who became famous in the 1800s for his stained glass windows and lamps.

MUSIC

Florida has a number of symphony orchestras. Three of the best-known are the Florida Philharmonic, the Jacksonville Symphony, and the New World Symphony. They perform for thousands of people each year.

Orlando Pilots and Cartoon Characters

Airplane pilots in Orlando have some strange sayings. Any plane arriving at Orlando International Airport must use one of two approach methods with funny names. One approach method is named GOOFY TWO. Another is called MINNIE TWO. They are named after the Disney characters Goofy and Minnie Mouse, since Walt Disney helped make Orlando famous.

Businesses and Products

Florida's most famous product is orange juice. Florida farmers grow more citrus than any place in the world except Brazil. Florida grows most of the world's grapefruit.

ORANGE JUICE

Several businesses in Florida make orange juice. Tropicana buys one of every four oranges grown in Florida every year, and makes more than one million gallons of juice each day. The Minute Maid Company also uses hundreds of thousands of Florida oranges each year.

SUGARCANE

Florida grows more sugarcane than any other state. Sugarcane grows in tall stalks. The sugar you find in the grocery is often made from sugarcane. Florida's largest sugarcane grower is U.S. Sugar, in Clewiston. This company is the nation's largest maker of sugar from sugarcane. U.S. Sugar turns out 1,600,000,000 pounds of raw sugar each year. U.S. Sugar also owns 29,000 acres of Florida orange groves.

Factories squeeze Florida oranges into juice, which is then put in cartons and bottles and shipped to stores all across the United States.

This raw sugar is being processed in a factory. When finished, it will look like the white sugar you buy in the grocery store.

OTHER PRODUCTS

Florida produces seafood, vegetables, and plants. Workers catch grouper and shrimp and sell them around the country. Farmers grow tomatoes, bell peppers, and sweet corn and ship them north in the winter, when the weather is too cold for northern farmers to grow crops. Florida has many nurseries, which are farms for shrubs and houseplants. Florida grows more houseplants than any other state.

You may not know that Florida, with its many cattle ranches, is a major contributor to the national beef and dairy industry. Florida's mines produce 75 percent of the **phosphate** used in this country. Each year, more than 33 million tons of phosphate rock are **extracted.** And Tarpon Springs, Florida, is famous for harvesting sea sponges.

SPACE EXPLORATION

The Kennedy Space Center on Florida's east coast makes the state a leader in the **aerospace** industry. Scientists and researchers there are continually developing new ideas that will help us explore space more thoroughly. The center also teaches us about our space exploration history and the future of the **International Space Station.**

Attractions and Landmarks

Almost everyone knows about Florida's most famous attractions, like Walt Disney World. However, there are many other things to see and do in the Sunshine State.

HISTORIC LANDMARKS

The Castillo de San Marcos is in St. Augustine, the oldest European city in the United States. The Castillo is a fort built by Spanish **conquerors** in the late 1600s from coquina. Coquina is a local stone made mostly of seashells. The Spanish used coquina because there was a lot of it near the seashore, where St. Augustine is located.

The thick walls of the Castillo de San Marcos in St. Augustine kept out many attackers over the years.

Vizcaya was built in 1916 near Miami. A man named James Deering wanted it to look like an Italian palace. He

filled his home with valuable furniture, art, and musical instruments. Today, you can walk through Vizcaya, which is now a museum.

Vizcaya is one of the oldest buildings in Miami. It has large gardens, including a maze garden.

PARKS

Florida boasts many outdoor attractions, including more than 130 state parks. Some of these, such as the John Pennekamp Coral Reef State Park in Key Largo, showcase

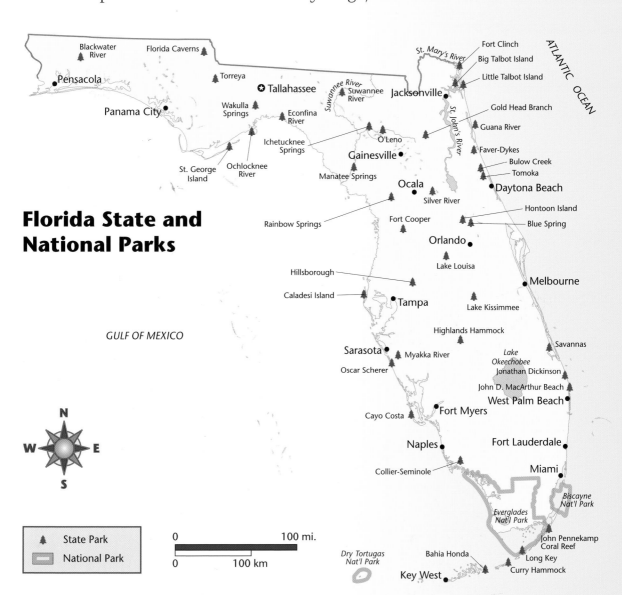

Florida State and National Parks

Blackwater River
Florida Caverns
Pensacola
Panama City
Torreya
Wakulla Springs
St. George Island
Ochlocknee River
Econfina River
Ichetucknee Springs
Manatee Springs
Rainbow Springs
Suwannee River
Tallahassee
Suwannee River
O'Leno
Gainesville
Ocala
Silver River
Fort Cooper
St. Mary's River
Fort Clinch
Big Talbot Island
Little Talbot Island
Jacksonville
St. John's River
Gold Head Branch
Guana River
Faver-Dykes
Bulow Creek
Tomoka
Daytona Beach
Hontoon Island
Blue Spring
Orlando
Lake Louisa
ATLANTIC OCEAN
Hillsborough
Caladesi Island
Tampa
Lake Kissimmee
Melbourne
Highlands Hammock
Sarasota
Oscar Scherer
Myakka River
Lake Okeechobee
Jonathan Dickinson
John D. MacArthur Beach
West Palm Beach
Savannas
Cayo Costa
Fort Myers
Naples
Collier-Seminole
Fort Lauderdale
Miami
Biscayne Nat'l Park
Everglades Nat'l Park
John Pennekamp Coral Reef
Long Key
Curry Hammock
Dry Tortugas Nat'l Park
Bahia Honda
Key West
GULF OF MEXICO

N
W E
S

State Park
National Park

0   100 mi.
0   100 km

Florida's **environment**. This park was the first underwater state park in the country. Here, visitors can see the variety of coral found in Florida's waters. Other parks teach about important historical events that took place in Florida. For example, the Natural Bridge Battlefield Historic State Park in Tallahassee tells the story of one of the only **Civil War** battles fought in Florida, and serves as a **memorial** to troops who died during the war.

WATER

Some of Florida's attractions take advantage of all the water. Some people enjoy riding airboats in the Everglades.

Airboats are wide, metal boats with flat bottoms, and are powered by huge fans. Many airboat rides are given by Florida Native Americans.

Other people enjoy parasailing. Parasailers are strapped into a large parachute and attached to a boat by a rope. As the boat moves faster, the parasailer rises into the air.

Other unique water attractions include Marineland, on Florida's east coast, where visitors can swim with dolphins; Silver Springs, near Ocala, which offers glass-bottomed boat rides; and Seaworld in Orlando, the world's most famous marine park.

Many marine animals perform for the audiences at Seaworld. Pilot whales (left) perform spectacular stunts to delight the crowds.

KENNEDY SPACE CENTER

The Kennedy Space Center at Cape Canaveral Air Force Station launched the spacecraft that put humans on the moon in 1969 for the very first time in history. The Center continues to send astronauts into space today, most of whom are working on the **International Space Station.**

GARDENS

Bok Tower, a national historic landmark in Lake Wales, offers 157 acres of woodland gardens. Fairchild **Tropical** Garden in Coral Gables is one of the world's most respected **botanic gardens,** and is an international leader in tropical plant research. Cypress Gardens, in central Florida, has several of the largest flower displays in the world.

America's Venice

Did you know that Venice, Italy, is famous for its **canals?** Well, the southern Florida city of Fort Lauderdale likes to call itself the "Venice of America." Fort Lauderdale has 165 miles of waterways. You can ride water taxis and other boats around the canals of Fort Lauderdale, just as you can in Venice.

Buildings and Structures

Many of Florida's famous buildings and structures are near the ocean. One of these is the Seven Mile Bridge, in the Florida Keys, which allows cars to travel between Marathon and Bahia Honda. It is exactly seven miles long. Another well-known bridge is the Sunshine Skyway Bridge, which connects St. Petersburg and Bradenton. This bridge is tall enough to allow large ships to pass beneath.

LIGHTHOUSES

The Cape Florida Lighthouse in Key Biscayne is the oldest surviving lighthouse in Florida. In 1836, after the start of the **Second Seminole War,** the lighthouse was attacked by Seminoles who didn't want settlers in that area. The keeper of the lighthouse was wounded, but was later rescued by the United States Navy.

You can climb to the top of the lighthouse in St. Augustine. It was built in 1824, but a newer lighthouse was built in the same place in 1874 and still stands today.

One of the most famous lighthouses in Florida is the St. Augustine Lighthouse. You have to climb 219 steps to get to the top.

Map of Florida

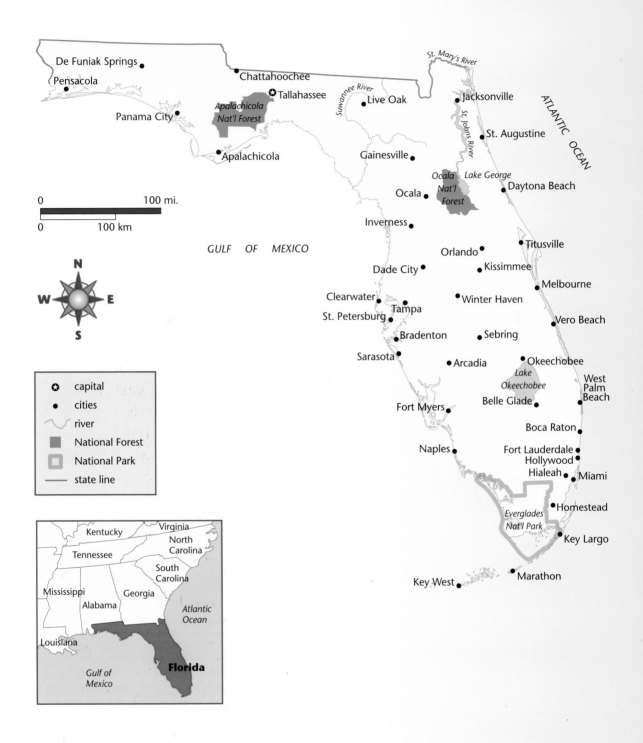

De Funiak Springs
Pensacola
Chattahoochee
Panama City
Apalachicola Nat'l Forest
Tallahassee
Apalachicola
Suwannee River
Live Oak
St. Mary's River
Jacksonville
St. Johns River
St. Augustine
ATLANTIC OCEAN
Gainesville
Ocala Nat'l Forest
Lake George
Daytona Beach
Ocala
Inverness
GULF OF MEXICO
Orlando
Kissimmee
Titusville
Melbourne
Dade City
Winter Haven
Clearwater
Tampa
St. Petersburg
Bradenton
Sebring
Vero Beach
Sarasota
Arcadia
Okeechobee
Lake Okeechobee
West Palm Beach
Fort Myers
Belle Glade
Boca Raton
Naples
Fort Lauderdale
Hollywood
Hialeah
Miami
Homestead
Everglades Nat'l Park
Key Largo
Key West
Marathon

0   100 mi.
0   100 km

N
W   E
S

Legend

⊗ capital
• cities
〰 river
▨ National Forest
▢ National Park
— state line

Kentucky
Virginia
Tennessee
North Carolina
South Carolina
Mississippi
Georgia
Alabama
Atlantic Ocean
Louisiana
Florida
Gulf of Mexico

Glossary

aerospace having to do with space

ancestor person from whom you are descended

appeal to ask a higher court for a different decision than that given by a lower court

artifact object created and used by humans long ago

awning piece of cloth or metal that is spread over a door or window to offer protection from the sun or rain

big game large animal, such as a buffalo, hunted for food or sport

botanic garden large garden, sometimes indoors, with many types of plants

cabinet group of people, either elected or appointed, that help run a government

canal waterway, built by people, that looks like a calm river. Canals can be used to ship goods or people to different locations.

circumference distance around a globe

Civil War U.S. war fought from 1861 to 1865 between northern and southern states

conqueror person who comes to an area from another land and takes control from people already living there

continental all U.S. states except for Alaska and Hawaii

culture beliefs, goals, art, music, and history shared by a particular group of people

currency paper and coin money

drama play about a serious subject

environment land, water, and air around us

equator imaginary horizontal line that divides Earth's Northern Hemisphere from the Southern Hemisphere

exhibit display in a museum

extract to take out

federal government United States government in Washington, D.C., which has responsibility for all states

immigrant person who moves from one country to another country

influence to affect

income tax money that the government takes out of a worker's paycheck

inheritance tax money paid to the government for any goods or money that a person receives from someone who has died

International Space Station large station being built in space with the cooperation of sixteen different countries. When complete, the station will weigh one million pounds and host an international crew of seven people who will live and work in space for up to six months at a time.

latitude measurement, in degrees, of distance to the north or south of the equator

legislature group of people who make laws

longitude measurement, in degrees, of distance to the east or west of the prime meridian

memorial location that has been preserved to honor the memory of an event

phosphate material mined from the earth that is used in fertilizers

prime meridian imaginary vertical line that divides Earth's Eastern Hemisphere from the Western Hemisphere

prop object used onstage during a play or production

Second Seminole War second in a series of three wars between the United States Army and the Seminoles of Florida. The army wanted to force the Seminoles out of Florida so settlers could live on their land; the Seminoles did not want to leave. The Second Seminole War took place from 1835 to 1842.

soil upper layer of earth in which plants grow

specimen plant or animal— thought to be a good representation of its type—that is studied by scientists

spiritual type of song that has to do with religion

surrealist artist or author whose work is very dreamlike

thrive flourish

tropical describes an area where hot sun and lots of rain help many plants and animals live

truce agreement to end a war or conflict

More Books to Read

Bruun, Erik. *Florida*. N.Y.: Black Dog & Leventhal Publishers, Inc., 2002.

Italia, Bob. *Florida Marlins*. Edina, Minn.: ABDO Publishing Co., 1997.

Lantz, Peggy S. and Wendy A. Hale. *The Florida Water Story: From Raindrops to the Sea*. Sarasota, FL: Pineapple Press, Inc., 1998.

McAuliffe, Emily. *Florida Facts and Symbols*. Minnetonka, Minn.: Capstone Press, 1998.

Somervill, Barbara A. *Florida*. Danbury, Conn.: Children's Press, 2001.

Index

About the Author

Bob Knotts is an author and playwright who lives near Fort Lauderdale, Florida. He has published 24 novels and nonfiction books for both young readers and adults. He also writes for several top national magazines.